THE ROLE OF INDIAN MEDIA IN COVERING CRIMES: A CRITICAL ANALYSIS

VOLUME 2, ISSUE 1 OF BRAIN BOOSTER ARTICLES

SHASHWATA SAHU

Contents

Preface

"Start writing, no matter what. The water does not flow until the faucet is turned on".

-Louis L'Amour

Hundreds of students and professors are contributing their work to Brain Booster Articles, we are here to provide ample information about Law and Contemporary issues. Our aim is to provide a platform for today's generation to express their views and ideas on law and contemporary law.

Author

Shashwata Sahu

CHAPTER ONE

ABSTRACT

"There is no democracy without journalism"

- **Mr. Scott Pelley**

In the present era, the media is a powerful weapon. Only when Governments utilize this weapon wisely, it strengthens the country's national peace and tends to make people's lives easier and it allows the government to directly address people's pain. Governments should demonstrate the media's openness and seriousness to the entire populace. India is a democratic nation with three main pillars: the legislature, the executive, and the independent judiciary. Without a doubt, the media is the fourth pillar in Indian democracy, protecting the independence of other organs and providing a check and balance on their actions. This paper seeks to examine the role of the media in criminal investigations, particularly the importance of not conducting a parallel criminal trial well with the judiciary. This legal document is divided into eight halves. The first portion seeks to understand the media trial's definition, types, and numerous roles of the media. Then, the second and third parts are going to familiarize the reader with a relevant literature review. Later, other incidents in which a media trial occurred and had a broad impact on public opinion and judicial decision has been discussed. This paper also admires how private media players impact the public's perspective of the media through their functions.

KEYWORDS: Democracy, India, Media, Crime, Media trial

CHAPTER TWO

INTRODUCTION

Meaning

The definition of media in the dictionary is to disseminate information to the broader public as well as to connect the world on a common platform. In simple terms, media serves as a link between citizens and government, allowing them to convey their concerns through their source materials. In the twenty-first century, the media is essential to promoting national peace and expressing the concerns of ordinary people. Giving the media more independence will help to improve the nation's human rights condition. Generally we glorified the role of the independent media like a "watchdog".

The print media, electronic media, hybrid software, social media, and application mode like the internet, FM radio and android TV are all examples of media that can be used to communicate with the general audience. The primary responsibility of an advertising agency is to identify the most appropriate media instruments for effectively communicating the advertising message to the common persons.

As a result, it is crucial for the ad agency to:

- Keep up with the latest trends
- Monitor the development of new media tools
- Conduct regular study to determine which instrument has the greatest impact.
- Examine the advantages and disadvantages of media companies.

The media can be divided into four categories:

- Print media (Journals, Newspaper, Magazines)
- Cinema & Video advertising
- Electronic media (Television industry)

- Social media (via online media or different social media platforms)

Role of media -

In a different light, the media play a different role. We will focus on various common media components in this section.

- A source of information.
- 0Represent the government in a positive light.
- Raise some serious public-policy problems.
- Between the general population and the government, there is a mediator.
- Creating a platform that brings individuals from all around the world together.

"According to **Walter Cronkite** Freedom of the Press is democracy and the court was wise enough to understand and analyze the relationship between Democracy and Press."

Media has become a powerful channel of communication that promotes the transmission of knowledge, the debunking of false beliefs, the correction of wrong or outdated information, and the sculpting of public opinion, all of these can have an impact on international politics. Throughout history, the media has been used by the people to fight against tyranny. The media has played a vital part in transforming feudal cultures into modern society all across the world, with the greatest visible effects in the world's westernmost regions.

Because of certain recent scandals, the media's role has now been highlighted. The media's function in today's society is evolving. Media began to spread various beliefs, dividing the populace into Hindus vs. Muslims, Majority vs. Minority, Male vs Female, and Nationalists vs. Anti-nationalists. In addition, media companies are turning the media into a business. As a result of this, the media has ruined their picture in the eyes of society.

CHAPTER THREE

CONCEPTUALIZATION

The press has evolved into a "Jantaki Adalat," or "open court," and has begun meddling with judicial proceedings. By respecting the key concepts of "presumption of innocence until proven guilty" and "guilt beyond a reasonable doubt," the media actually forgot the distinction between the accused and the convict.

A second investigation, known as a media trial, is currently being followed. In addition to the investigation, it requires developing the opinion of the public against any suspect or accused well before the Court takes control of the case. As a consequence, the public is misled, and the accused, who really should be deemed innocent, is assumed guilty, with full access to all of his rights and liberties.

When anotable case is presented before the Court, the populace's interest is stirred. The media, comprising newspapers, television and news websites, begin releasing their perceptions of the facts in order to stay updated with the recent exciting news. In India, investigative journalism is not banned. "Media Trial" or "Trial by Media" referred to as the effects of media coverage on a person via newspapers and television in creating a perception of innocence or guilt even before the court of law renders its judgement.

Debates in the media are nowadays causing more misunderstanding among the general people. In this style, they begin an opinion-based reporting show in which they attempt to change the public perception of a certain incident. In this collection of viewpoints, they created primetime shows, in which they called certain senseless panellists in the studio and initiated a debate on the big headlines in which they are obtaining views of panellists on the news. Finally, the audience should be puzzled as to what point they are trying to prove with that discussion. This shift in the media industry occurred after private media companies were allowed to participate in journalism and began producing news as a business.

They manipulated the information and always sought to sell the news without verifying the accuracy of comments that affected people's lives and the freedoms they were granted under the constitution. The Honourable Chief Justice of India, Shri N. V. Ramana, has commented on the television debates: "Debates on TV are creating more pollution than everybody. They don't understand that statements are taken out of context. Everyone has their agenda. The media did not present some sensitive news about a celebrity who committed suicide in recent times. They forgot to follow the guidelines of the press councilof India."

CHAPTER FOUR

REVIEW OF RELEVANT LITERATURE

The role of the media in present times was discussed in a "**Blog (ssim institute) in 2019"**[1], which indicated that the influence of mass media in the present era is just like an ideal thing that has ever happened. Our lives are shaped by the media, and that takes a lot of time and effort. And they have the ability to control the human mind, so anything they generate for the viewers will be followed without question. A study exposes how different sorts of media influence society, including how fake news affects society, and how technology nowadays puts media in our hands.

In "**International journals of law (volume 4 issue 2 2021)**" there is a piece of research about trials by media which reveals that the term "trial by media" was coined a little quicker than anticipated in the late 20thcentury or early 21st century to describe the effects of broadcast and print coverage on a person's reputation by instilling a general feeling of guilt or innocence previously, or just after, a court judgement of guilt or innocence. During recent times, there have been numerous instances of unethical activity on the part of the media. An accused's prosecution has ended and a verdict has already been determined even before the Court makes a decision.

According to a study of "**Journal of criminal justice (volume 17, issue 4, 1989)**", it was described that the media outlets engage in investigative journalism in order to create drama for their viewers. They display the entire scene from a different perspective in order to shift the viewer's perception. The most essential issue is that such instruments are used by powerhouses to create propaganda toward anything.

In a scholarly article of "**Giles Gherson (Canadian speaker) the role of media and public perception(2004)**"[2], a study illustrates how the media affects public perceptions of national issues. A regulated material produced by a media firm according to their founder, who coordinated with the government and other organisations to modify the public image of any policy, human rights violation or agenda issues. Currently, the media does an insufficient and uncomplicated job of covering and interpreting every country's national affairs, and major events in each state are lowered to little more than headlines over borders.

According to a study of **"Belinda middleweek (feminist media studies (volume 17, issue -3) 2017"**, the agreement among the people, media, and some other administrated persons in Azaria is to blame for sensationalist reporting in the case of a woman guilty of the death of her daughter in the month of August in 1980, which was viewed as a media trial.

Inside the article titled **"Media Trials in India: A Judicial View to Administration-2021"**[3], the author **Vishwajeet Deshmukh** interprets what the Supreme Court stated: "There is a need to strike a balance between the judiciary, the executive, the parliament, and the court, which has a duty to maintain this balance between three organs of democracy from the bench to the media, which is called actual function of journalism," as we have seen recent times in the particular instance of a film industry actor's suicide. Additionally, the ruling of the High Court of Bombay should not be seen as a remedy. Following and enforcing the Bombay High Court's authorised guidelines will become the ultimate achievement. As new technologies and accessibility of the information become available, the "Modern Foundation of Indian Media Trials" jurisprudence will expand.

As per the "**200th Report of law commission of India (trial by media, august 2006),**" [4]the period (2005-2009) is known as the "Golden Period of Journalism," because it was during this time that media institutions reached their peak in terms of journalism. They began many projects, including investigative journalism as well as sting operations targeting senior government officials. Various questions regarding running propaganda against the administration were brought up in the media as a result of this. "The Ministry of Law and Justice then convened a suo moto hearing, which was presided over by Judge M. JAGANNADHA RAO, Chairman of the Law Commission of India." Identifying that, since media freedom is not absolute, media professionals in electronic and print media should be adequately informed well about purview of the "fundamental right to freedom of speech and expression, as well as what is and is not permitted to be published under the right to freedom of speech and expression."

In "**G.N.Ray (Media Ethics) 2007**", the "Chairman of the Press Council of India'' gave a speech regarding the importance of media ethics in today's world. "Let excellent thoughts come to us from all sides," says the Rigveda's everlasting word, which was given several millennia ago and indicates the freedom of expression. The right to express thoughts has served as the core principle in the construction of the contemporary democratic tower, which is constructed on the foundations indicated above. Over age, the actual form of this phrase, "journalism," has grown in power. This has become a sought-after profession amongtodaysmodern career-conscious youth, so I am confident that I would be going to meet an up-and-coming bunch of participants here today, most of whom will unquestionably earn a place among the leading media outlets in the years ahead. The main objective of journalism is to provide the general population with unbiased, fair, decent news, accurate comments, opinions, and insights on topics of public interest.

In "**Law commission, consultation paper -cum questionnaire on undercover sting operations**", Technology gives a multitude of opportunities to intrude into a person's private and professional relationships, according to a set of standards created for the media about undercover sitting investigations. The media is trying to make good use of this technical opportunity to perform "Sting Operations (SO)" to root out corruption, exploitation, immorality, and rule of law abuses by individuals in positions of authority, essential individuals, and people in business, well with help of private organisations. Furthermore, in certain high-profile criminal cases, the media has been compelled to exploit the emotions of the victims and sensationalise the incidents for economic gain by conducting SO and airing it constantly on television. It has a tendency to shift public opinion inside one direction, well to the dismay of law enforcement agencies. There have been several cases where quick SMS polls have indeed been utilised to judge guilt or innocence. "Parallel media procedures in a criminal case pending in a court of law might produce a strong picture of responsibility in the public consciousness, potentially affectinga fair trial and open verdict, which is a constitutional protection."

CHAPTER FIVE

AIMS & OBJECTIVES

- To know the origins of media houses conducting a parallel criminal trial and court and concluding that a person was found guilty.
- To investigate how media house ownership obstructs independent work and why they occasionally neglect to adhere to their constitutional obligations.
- To answer why do media companies forget their constitutional responsibilities as the media in the pursuit of profit?
- To verify how does the government combat false news processes in social, print, and electronic media?

CHAPTER SIX

THEORETICAL FRAMEWORK

There are a number of famous hypotheses that fall under the heading of "media influences," as well as a number of core assumptions. To go further into detail on each one would be beyond the scope of this text. Here's an overview of some of the most popular theories.

George Gerbner's cultivation theory[1]is based on the idea that people's perception is the most essential factor. Viewers of television and online platforms perceive this to be true. After that, they communicate those viewpoints to their family, friends, employees, and so forth, forming a communication chain. And all these shared thoughts have an impact on one's decision-making. For example, if a person cannot make a choice to whom to consider voting for in an election, his friends, family, or supervisor will force him to follow their opinions. Today's television content is degrading in terms of quality; they've started airing more violent content, which has an impact on their viewers' lifestyles.

As per **dependency theory**[2], there is a critical link connecting the media and their viewers because media relies on TRP ratings, which determine which station has the most viewers. This audience paves the path for funding for similar media outlets. They must obtain the majority of advertisement contracts in order to make cash. According to this hypothesis, media outlets create the content that their audiences desire because if they don't, they will fall behind in the industry. Dependency is a connection in which one party's fulfilment of needs or goals is contingent on the availability of resources.

[1]https://www.verywellmind.com/cultivation-theory-5214376

[2]https://www.academia.edu/9834996/Media_Dependency_Theory_in_Use

CHAPTER SEVEN

RESEARCH METHODOLOGY

This research is based on an examination of academic literature that aided in the formulation of the research topic. The analysis presented in this paper is collected from secondary sources gathered from scholarly journals, reports from various agencies, periodicals, media coverage, and interactions with advocates. The research is completely qualitative. This paper has tried to look at how the media can influence court judgments and proceedings. Addressing how media coverage impacts court proceedings and outcomes, this article seeks to analyse two distinct elements. Firstly, examine how the media influences judges‘ and the public's choices and perspectives. Secondly, investigated the structure and personality of the judges' and public's reasons. This article thoroughly studied a number of factors to ensure that the methods were correct and studied the patterns of how to cover court events correctly and how the media presents the reports on the judiciary. This study also examined the media's effect on the bench, and how that view affects the outcomes of court hearings and rulings.

CHAPTER EIGHT

FINDINGS

The findings in this extensive analysis are based on specific circumstances in which the media runs a parallel criminal trial as well as the courtroom. They are often active in bringing justice to the victims and their family, and other times they are involved in ruining the character of the individual who has been declared acquitted by the court. This paper has utilised an easy research technique to analyse the data. The model was created to solve two fundamental questions: trace the roots of the media operating a parallel open trial system and also other elements responsible for the media's autonomy being compromised, and how media trials profoundly affected the Indian criminal court system. To finalise the work, the author has relied on her own experience, knowledge, and also the perspectives of other researchers.

1. **Case of Sheena Bohra's murder** -

According to various Youtube channels, victim Sheena Bora was an executive of Mumbai Metro who had been reported missing in the month of April, 2012. Several persons were captured by police on suspicions of kidnapping and murdering her, and then flaming her body after three months of her missing. The involved individuals were her stepfather, mother and driver of her mother. Khanna and Rai confessed that they have kidnapped and murdered her, and disposed her body in a fire. But as per Mukerjea, Sheena Bora was still alive and well there in the USA.

As per the strimming videos, big segments of the media would focus on the suspect's personal life and broadcast personal information about them that had little to do with the accusations. This involves delving into aspects of the accused's personality and personal lives that have nothing to do well with crimes they are accused of committing. The media has already presumptively assumed that Bhora's mother was the guilty of the murder her own daughter. Based only on information that builds a sequence of events from the moment she was apprehended, well before her murder trial had even began.

In a scholarly essay titled "Media and Democracy - Legal Perspective," a research scholar who is an assistant professor of law, bemoaned that the media unfairly "pierced the personal lives of the participants" in the specific instance of Bora. The author states that the character and personal affairs elements that the media exploited to bring public attention to the plight were not legally relevant to the criminal investigation. He accused the media of putting his family on trial in front of the public. In a diverse media business, the media has been accused of altering facts to garner attention. The author also accused the media for extensively reporting court cases "by disseminating material and opinions that are manifestly harmful to the interests of the parties involved in pending litigation before the courts".

2. Murder case of Priyadarshini Mattoo -

In 1996, Priyadarshini Mattoo was found murdered and raped in her own house, as has been documented in several Youtube clips. Santosh Kumar Singh was declared gulty of murder and rape by the Delhi High Court in 2006 and overturned his acquittal by the trial court. The court found him guilty and sentenced him to death. A year later, Santosh Kumar Singh's death sentence was modified to life imprisonment by the Supreme Court of India. The films clearly demonstrate that the acquittal provoked enormous public outrage, which was widely covered by the media. Despite general perception that Santosh was accused for the death of Mattoo, investigative reporters went out to find the grounds for the court's order to acquit him.

The media conducted a thorough investigation and conducted several sting operations that were not presented to the trial court. The "Central Bureau of Investigation (CBI), India's top investigation agency", has filed an appeal even against the accused's acquittal, citing new evidence discovered by the media. The case was retried by the high court, which overturned Singh's acquittal and sentenced him to death. After seeing the films, we came to the conclusion that the press guaranteed that justice was served in this case, albeit after a long delay. The media contributed to the acquittal by filling up critical gaps that already had previously led towards the acquittal.

The press has reappeared as a "public court," also referred as "Janata Adalat." It has started interfering with judicial proceedings to the extent where it now makes its own decision in front of the court. They wrote all of the concepts, regulations, and recommendations on the back. In peril, they omitted to obey the basic golden rules of "presumption of innocence until proven guilty" and "guilt beyond a reasonable doubt." The media's involvement in the Mattoo case, as per the filmmakers, aided the high court by securing justice.

3. **Aarushi Talwar murder case** -

We saw numerous of Aarushi Talwar's murder mystery films, all of which are still unresolved. Her doctor's parents are accused of murdering her. She was slain at her home in May of 2008. The films demonstrated that the case received a lot of media attention and curiosity. Because the outrageous claims levelled against the murdered girl were made public, the incident became a media phenomenon.

The murder suspects were acquitted by the court, alleging that the prosecution has really failed to present sufficient evidence against them. This also reprimanded the media for doing minimal investigations into the crime.So when the media takes this case to ensure that the victim receives justice, the court is required to consider the aforementioned considerations. They mandated that the investigative agency perform extensive study within a certain amount of time. Another researcher, a law assistant professor, attempted to claim that the media emphasised this case solely on the basis of assumptions, not scientific research mostly on subject, and diverted the particular instance from murder to other perspective, leading viewers to presume that his side story is correct and reasonable – "A Valuable Means to Justice".

Many television stations purposefully distorted information regarding the case in order to get more viewers, producing a great deal of confusion. The media is once again doing something excessively similar to what he did previously. They dug into the accused's personal life, exposing their true identity in front of every audience, and began to earn public sympathy. As a result, the accused has been subjected to public humiliation on numerous occasions. The media "made every effort to promote features of illicit relationships, adultery, fornication, mystery, and honour killing" to combat the success of daily soaps.

The media was eager to go to such depths that it supplied unsubstantiated information that cast doubt on the depiction of the murdered girl and her family. The real image of media crimes is portrayed in the films and stories as harming the court's verdict, meaning that justice was not achieved. The court admonished the press, trying to point out the media's impact over judges.

4. **Murder case of Ruchika Girhotra -**

I saw three videos regarding the victim's incident on the internet, each of which displayed a police inspector general sexually assaulting Ruchika. But upon lodging a complaint only against the inspector, she, including family, and friends were faced with ongoing harassment by police forces. As an outcome of the harassment, she died by suicide. Because of our criminal justice system, that inspector was eventually accused of molestation of the victim numerous years later. The defendant was sentenced to six months' imprisonment by the bench. The CBI appealed the decision, asking for the sentence to be lengthened to two years. Then Chandigarh District Court increased the sentence to one & a half years. The policeman was granted bail by the Highest Court in the land, which affirmed a previous prison sentence of six months. The videos persuaded me that perhaps the media sensationalized the matter in order to ensure that Ruchika was given justice. Because of the weakened criminal justice system, witnesses became hostile once again, and the offender was acquitted. After the media raised a question about the criminal justice process, the case was revisited. Since the press was so interested in this issue, they had previously conducted extensive research upon that victim, the accused, and the witnesses who were finally presented in the case. In an article titled "Trial by Media and Criminal Justice Administration, Suman and Abhishek (2014) concluded that the media played a vital role in ensuring justice for the victim's family."

5. **Murder case of Jayendra Saraswathi -**

In Bharat, religion is the most important thing that people follow, so religious representatives become public figures who are rigorously followed by their followers. "In this particular instance, a manager in the Varadarajan temple enclosure worked for JayendraSaraswati. He was the one in command. VijayendraSaraswati& His Holiness were seized as a result of a report filed by investigative journalist Dhanasekaran Prakash. The assassination of the manager's manager, Jayendra Saraswathi Swamigal, was a key suspect." As per the investigation, this manager made many complaints about all of the accused. In the finale, twenty-four people were charged and prosecuted for the manager's murder. All twenty-four defendants were acquitted by the trial court, which ruled that the evidence for them was inadequate to convict them. The media impacted the public's impression of the case, making it impossible to analyse the evidence properly. The claim that Jayendra Saraswathi Swamigal was indeed the murderer had been widely reported in the media. The defendants, however, were acquitted by the high courts of Andhra Pradesh and Madras, as well as the Apex Court. The courts chastised the media for their reporting of the case and rushed to rule on Jayendra Saraswathi Swamigal well before courts had reached a decision.

6. **Some recent incident -**

"In 2018, in wake of the #MeToo movement in India, Journalist Priya Ramani had made allegations of sexual misconduct against the then Minister of State for External Affairs MJ Akbar through a tweet. Ramani was acquitted by Delhi court in a criminal defamation case filed by former Union Minister M.J. Akbar for accusing him of sexual misconduct. The court said that a woman has the right to express her grievances even after decades and that the right of reputation cannot be protected at the cost of the right to dignity. (**Mobashar Jawed Akbar v. Priya Ramani on 17 February, 2021**)."[1]

"**Vinod Dua V. The Union of India** has upheld the virtue of freedom of speech and expression and understanding the freedom required for journalism to perform its duty as the fourth pillar of democracy."[2]

"The Aurangabad bench of the Bombay high court recently issued additional restraints on print and electronic media to ensure that the identity of rape or child abuse survivors is not disclosed indirectly by publishing details of their parents, address or name of school."[3]

Legal Perspective of Media Trial -

When judges are exposed to media trials, they may become swayed by the information and make unjust decisions. The Supreme Court ruled in "**In Re: PCSen**" [4]that "the effect of the publication on justice should take precedence over the publication's objective." In 2007, India's Chief Justice remarked that judges should follow the law and rule on every issue that comes before them, regardless of how well-known the case is. Other than the so-called wrongdoer's destroyed reputation, even witnesses are harassed because they have been questioned continuously by both the media and the government. When the witness's identity is made public, the harassment escalates, and they make every effort to disavow themselves.

The Supreme Court ruled in **"Reliance Petrochemicals v. Indian Express Newspapers Bombay (Pvt.) Ltd."** that courts cannot be persuaded by public opinion or the journalism on a particular issue. In the case of **"Ankul Chandra Pradhan v. UOI,"** the Apex Court declared that publicity is not a basis for refusal of a fair trial. The SC established in the case of **"State of Maharashtra v. Rajendra Jawanmal Gandhi"** that a media trial is also against the rule of law and might result in a miscarriage of justice. Judges should not cave to media pressure. Nonetheless, the media has also played a constructive influence. The Apex Court condemned an article that presented only one side of the story and cautioned the newspaper's editor against interfering with the administration of justice. "The High Court revived the case of **Santosh Kumar Singh v. State**[5], also known as the Priyadarshini Mattoo case, due to immense media pressure, and condemned the accused to death. Because he was the son of an Inspector General, the Trial Court had acquitted him."

In "**Sahara India Real Estate Corp. v. SEBI**,"[6]the SC was requested to draft appropriate rules for the media concerning sub judice cases. The court ruled that "a difficult balance had to be struck between the right to a fair trial and the right to freedom of expression, and that postponement orders would be the best remedy in that situation." The Court's refusal to file contempt cases stems from the right to FOSE. The judgment went on to say that the media serves as a channel between the public and the courts, whose rulings become the "Law of the Land" in the end. The Ruling went on to say that unique solutions are needed, "for neither the right to freedom of expression nor the right to fair trial must be compromised."

"In **Election Commission of India v MR Vijaya Bhaskar (2021)**, a division bench of Justices DY Chandrachud and MR Shah held that freedom of speech and expression under Article 19(1)(a) extends to reporting judicial proceedings in judicial institutions as well. Citizens have the right to know what transpires in judicial proceedings. The SC upheld the freedom of the media to report the oral observations and discussions made by judges and lawyers during a court proceeding. The court observed that freedom of media to report court proceedings was also a part of the process of augmenting the integrity of the judiciary and the cause of justice as a whole."[7]

A Study of Contempt of Court by Media[8] -

It requires a free media to perform its tasks correctly. However, it is important to note that the media does not have any special rights. While fighting for their freedom as granted in **Article -19(1), it is confined to Article -19(2)(a).** Judiciary do not launch contempt proceedings, except in exceptional situations, to allow the media to do its work. Even the "**1971-Contempt Act's Sections 3, 4, 5, 7, and 13**" provide guidance on where the boundary should be drawn between court procedures and media intervention.

The "**200th Law Commission Report**" (under title - "Trial by Media: Free Speech and Fair Trial Under Criminal Procedure Code, 1973") considered these issues as well, and made the following recommendations:

- To broaden the Act's scope and ambit the definition of "publication" was added.
- Arrest is to be considered the beginning of a case that is pending before the courts.
- Insertion of a new section that includes "Sections-2(c)(ii) and 2(c)(iii)" so that the method outlined in "Section 15(1)" of the Act is followed.
- Allow publishing postponement when it affects ongoing criminal procedures, but not when it impacts the reporting of cases that are still pending.

Article-129 gives the Supreme Court while Article-215 gives the High Courts the competence to regulate contempt of court. This indicates that, irrespective of the Act, the Court system are given such authority by the Constitution. This is not to say, that somehow the Act ought not be amended. The Act needs to be modified so that the concept of inherent jurisdiction can be articulated more thoroughly. It must be made abundantly clear that if a judgeinitiates contempt proceedings unless his name has been tarnished, he doesn't always sit on the bench during the proceedings. The Act provides for such a procedure, however it is not compulsory, and it should be.

The conditions under which contempt proceedings can be brought must be redefined such that they can be brought more for the benefit of the trial or justice. When a court is horrified by a certain action, tighter provisions are required since it appears that judges are readily provoked these days, that should not be the scenario. The Act must always be changed to make a clear distinction between the scandalization of the courts and the scorning of a single judge. "Defamation, not contempt, is the solution in the latter scenario."

The Act's definitions must also be clarified as soon as possible in order to provide clear guidelines as to what makes up contempt and what does not. A further thing to keep in mind is that pre-trial announcements are not subject to contempt actions. The media has taken advantage of this to a significant extent. The answer is to alter the Act to include this period as well. The Courts' own judgements have been contradicted as a result of this ambiguity. While this has the extra benefit of giving judges more discretionary power, decreasing the vagueness of the provisions would be the best remedy. Because things change so quickly, the Act must be amended to reflect the challenges and tribulations of modern life.

In the context of media publications which analyse court decisions, the Act appears to be applied appropriately. Nevertheless, when it comes to handling media trials, there are still certain gaps. There ought to be a dividing line made here. With the media's increased focus on TRP and journalism's transformation into a money-making machine, it's no longer just a media trial. The media has been doing almost the full job of the judiciary, from conducting investigations into specific cases to interviewing witnesses, analysing evidence, and even determining who the "real" criminal is.

It is just not imposing a sentence on the culprit because it lacks the powers to do so. And besides, who knows, if such heinous acts are not stopped today, something along those lines may emerge in the future. However, in this circumstance, modifying the Act is not a viable option. There must be a separate collection of rules also for media in the form of a code of conduct which specifies what acts are and are not acceptable.

The "Press Council of India's Norms of Journalistic Conduct" already exists India, but they do not impose punishments, and even if they did, they could not be implemented. Because the language of these standards is so soft, it is not an optimal answer. To allow the judiciary to do its job correctly, these norms must be modified to include tighter restrictions and enforcement procedures. Even the "Press Council of India's powers do not give it the authority to restrict pre-trial reporting." This, too, must be changed.

CHAPTER NINE

DISCUSSION ON THE FINDINGS

- The media is not being truthful about its role in democracy. Multiple factors have directly affected media independence in recent years, including ownership, media willingness to participate in business, trying to run media channels such as daily shops for TRP, as well as government interference in programme design; these are all the major reasons that have forced media houses to drive a parallel criminal trial alongside a court as well as pass a verdict just before court judgement.
- India is indeed one of the world's biggest media markets. The consolidation of media ownership, on either hand, shows that only a few individuals own and manage Indian media. Our research looks on media plurality as well as ownership arrangements. "This is an essential endeavour to increase media ownership transparency, which is fundamental to media's reputation and relationship with audiences," says the study accurately. The article implies that "this initiative will provide a useful data and resource foundation for future media studies in the country." Additionally, some of the most famous newspapers are influenced by political allegiances. Most media businesses, as shown in a research, have business and political connections, and the deeper one goes into regional and local levels, the more obvious and apparent the relationship develops. The interconnection between media, business, and politics that has resulted poses a severe threat to India's media freedom and pluralism. One option for the government to exercise political power is to praise or punish media outlets by providing or not assigning advertising, as several Indian states have recently done. This really is correct in our country; but it is even more critical at

the municipal and state levels, in which many media outlets depend on it to keep solvent and where transparency and accountability is not guaranteed. Political parties, in addition to the government, invest heavily in advertising, mostly with the ruling party, the Bharatiyajanata party, becoming one of the nation's top advertisers.[1]

- The financial situation of the media is catastrophic. To give a competent journalism service today, they require a significant budget. In India, many individuals refuse to buy newspapers or subscribe to news programmes. In comparison to other nations, the maximum price of a Hindi newspaper is Six rupees, the highest price of such an English newspaper is Ten rupees, and the charge of news channels via digital platforms is simply one rupee or a maximum of five rupees, which is far too cheap. And several media organisations rely just on advertising work of numerous government agencies to obtain income for spending expenses. These factors compelled media companies to participate in the profit-making process.

- Following a drop in the press freedom index, multiple instances of false information have created a buzz on social and electronic media. By trying to maintain a system which establishes the liability of social media platforms during an abusive environment, the government has agreed to amend its Information Technology rules in 2008. Whenever the government or a court directs these organizations to delete a post, they are required to comply within 36 hours.

[1]https://onlinelibrary.wiley.com/doi/10.1002/9781118541555.wbiepc156

CHAPTER TEN

CONCLUSION

After conducting a thorough investigation, we can conclude that the media has become a powerful tool for communicating a problem and thus it is extremely necessary in the twenty-first century because everybody is affected when their news is broadcast in the media, so think of a situation in which the media works tirelessly for the citizen's welfare. The media's freedom of speech and expression has been guaranteed by the Honorable Apex Court on numerous occasions, particularly COVID-19 periods. Journalists in the media widely highlighted nefarious things like Tablighi Jamaat and blamed them accountable for the virus's dissemination during the outbreak, and it was a really unprofessional style of reporting. Therefore, based on the above two instances, we may conclude that we require a responsible media that not only reports crime, but also knows how much they report as well as what their "LAXMAN REKHA" is. Numerous instances that we examined in our research paper, where the media did a great job and found hard evidence to really get the true accused punished and moreover raised a clear voice against influential people whose only flaw was their own reputation after the media raised their tone against them. Therefore, the only victim got justice, for instance –, a religious saga popularly called Ashram Bapu was punished only after the media brought up their voice against him, after that the victim got justice. Also, when well-known actor Sushant Singh Rajput commits suicide, the media unfairly targets his girlfriend, Ria Chakraborty. As a result, media outlets must recognise the fine line that must not be crossed in order for democracy to thrive.

Printed by Libri Plureos GmbH in Hamburg,
Germany